Answers for Sensitive People

Stories & Energetic Exercises to Live Life with More Harmony and Balance

Anne Steffen-Russo
with Kay Wise and Eric Russo

Answers for Sensitive People

"*Don't be fooled by the simplicity of the exercises. In this book, Anne offers powerful tools for personal empowerment and transformation.*"
—Susan Warner CEO

"*When we speak from our own experiences, our words have weight.* Answers for Sensitive People *uses experience and four short exercises to help us process our feelings and enjoy our journey. Ride On.*"
—John H. Wead Esq.

"*This is a valuable and user-friendly book. It is jam-packed with real life experiences and easy techniques that both adults and children can use to ease stress overload and encourage personal growth.*"
—Susan Eppley, Ed.D.,Psychologist

"*As an 18-year-old male in modern society, being sensitive is not widely accepted.Throughout my early childhood, I struggled with feelings of intense anxiety which led me to believe there was something wrong with me.Yet as I discovered that I could feel the emotions of others, I became bogged down by foreign energies in my space, as well as my own feelings of ostracism.Although I spent much of my formative youth in ignorance and denial of my own sensitivity, these exercises and the realization that I am not the only one with such a blessing have allowed me to discover myself in the truest of forms.Continual learning and growth (especially in the collegiate environment) through work like this has become paramount in my ability to lead a life full of joy, understanding, and love.*"
—C.J. college student

"*I wish this book had been around when I was growing up . . . to know I wasn't alone and give me the tools to manage my sensitivities. This will help so many people, at any stage of life.A clear, concise, straightforward and authentic presentation of what it means to be sensitive, coupled with simple, profound, easy to use tools for handling everyday life.*

Thank you to the authors for sharing their personal journeys. The true-life examples so mirrored my own life that I immediately connected with this book. "
—Carolyn Cental

Answers for Sensitive People

Stories & Energetic Exercises to Live Life with More Harmony and Balance

ANNE STEFFEN-RUSSO

with Kay Wise and Eric Russo

Illustrations by Ellen Ebel

**Answers for Sensitive People: Stories & Energetic Exercises
to Live Life with More Harmony and Balance**

by Anne Steffen-Russo, with Kay Wise and Eric Russo

Illustrations by Ellen Ebel

Copyright © 2012 www.EnergeticAnswers.com

ISBN-13: 978-0-692885-50-6

For further information, contact the publisher:

306 Greenup Street
Covington, KY 41011

Edited by Richard Hunt
Cover designed by Scott McGrew
Interior designed by Annie Long

PRINTED in the USA

Dedicated
to everyone
who has the courage
to grow

TABLE of CONTENTS

PREFACE

How this book came to be . . .

One day not long ago, a client contacted me because she was struggling with the intense pain and confusion that others around her were feeling. A sadness had overwhelmed her and she did not how to handle the situation. In her email, she asked if I knew of any books that could help her to understand these feelings. I replied, "No, let's write one!"

I was excited to be able to create this book along with two of my colleagues, bringing years of experience gathered from clients from all backgrounds. It's been a joy to also deliver exercises that are easy to learn and helpful for coping with day-to-day living.

Numerous clients have shared that when using these exercises daily, they are able to handle their emotions more skillfully. They begin to better understand their own feelings separate from those of others. Often, the client can feel more secure in their own space without interference from the pain or emotions of those around them. This can lead to greater personal fulfillment and compassion.

Most of my clients find me because I am highly sensitive myself. I have had to develop these tools to survive. I'm honored to share my knowledge in order to help others. This book is just the first of many that I want to share with readers who struggle with high sensitivity.

My wish for this book is that people see sensitivity as a strength, not a weakness. Although the exercises may be simple, thousands of people have noted their effectiveness

—Anne Steffen-Russo

Why a book for Sensitive People?

Have you ever thought that you feel too much? Have you been told that you are too sensitive? Perhaps someone once said that you're taking things "too seriously" and that you just need to "lighten up."

These examples are typical of the sensitive person. Being sensitive can feel like you are equipped with an extra set of emotions that can overwhelm and weigh you down.

Throughout this book are short sections describing what life can be like for a sensitive child, adolescent and adult. These personal recollections are offered as support and insight into what it means to be sensitive.

> *By the time I reached adolescence, I didn't know how to cope with growing social expectations and peer pressure. While I was popular as a child, I could not translate this into my teen years. I didn't know how to fit comfortably into my age group.*
>
> *I was hyper-aware that the things I thought and felt were not aligned with the majority of my peers. Kindness, imagination and sensitivity were the opposite of "cool." I turned to drugs, drinking, and reckless behavior. In truth, I was so miserable and unhappy most of the time I just wanted to die."* ~ Eric

When I was in second grade everyone wanted to be my friend. Some of the girls would fight over me. One day, a group of girls began tugging on both sides of me. I didn't know how to handle the competition over me nor how mean they could be to one another. I felt responsible for their meanness.

My pattern became one of trying to make everyone happy. By the time I reached puberty I was exhausted and depressed and wanted to lay on the couch a lot. Using these tools I found how to socialize with others, without feeling responsible for their behaviors.   ~ Shawn

You may have asked yourself:

Why do I have to feel this way?

Why does life have to be so hard?

Why am I different from others?

How can I relate to people yet not let them overwhelm or sadden me with their problems?

In this book, the first of four to be produced by **Energetic Answers.com,** we answer these questions and more. Also, at the conclusion of the book you will find fun and easy exercises that will help you become centered and stay balanced.

It's no coincidence that we call these tools Energetic Exercises. You move your physical body and exercise to keep your muscles and tendons fit and flexible. Energetic Exercises assist your energy to stay tuned up and in shape.

But like any muscle, you've got to use it to make it work. It's important for the sensitive person to keep their energy in shape by regularly practicing these exercises. In fact, for sensitive people, practicing regularly is essential. We suggest a minimum of once a day.

When I don't do the exercises presented in this book regularly, I feel out of balance. It feels like I am going around in circles, not getting anything accomplished. My partner notices I can easily lose my temper and become more irritable and depressed. Even though the exercises may seem simple, they help manage high levels of activity and stress in my life with greater ease. ~ Yvonnne

∞ ∞ ∞

The ideas and exercises presented here will get you in tune so that you can feel centered and balanced. Many sensitive people are abundantly resourceful, creative, imaginative and inspirational. These qualities are the foundation for a fulfilling and rich life. Celebrate your sensitivity! The Energetic Exercises offered in this book will help you do just that! Let's first define the qualities that make a person sensitive.

Are you a Sensitive Person?

The following list identifies key characteristics of the sensitive person. As you read it, note which ones apply to you.

- ❏ Feeling or being told you are "overemotional"
- ❏ Feeling overwhelmed by sadness, anxiety, grief, fear, etc.
- ❏ Feeling like you are lost and just don't fit in
- ❏ Feeling alienated or misunderstood
- ❏ Feeling alone and like an outsider looking in
- ❏ Feeling unsafe, insecure, shy, or stupid
- ❏ Feeling like you want to heal or fix everyone
- ❏ Feeling shut down
- ❏ Feeling the emotions of everyone around you
- ❏ Feeling invalidated and invisible
- ❏ Sensitive to medicines, foods, smells & environment
- ❏ Sensitive to driving
- ❏ Sensitive to large crowds or groups of people
- ❏ Highly allergenic

It's uncomfortable for me to drive a car. I take in the noise, movement and energy of all the people passing by. I feel a lot of anxiety, especially in bad weather with snow or rain. I pick up on the emotions of other drivers who may be anxious or stressed. ~ Anne

You may have known from a young age that you were sensitive. Perhaps it emerged sometime later in your life. Utilizing the tools here offers solutions for navigating sensitivity. Some families nurtured and managed sensitivity. Some families ignored it. Some of us were perhaps even punished for being a sensitive child.

When does confusion begin?

Where do core behaviors come from? Many of these "patterns" are established in childhood. As a sensitive child, growing up can be confusing. You may remember asking yourself: "Why doesn't everyone feel the way I do?"

If you did not learn how to manage your emotions as a teenager and young adult, it might cause dysfunctional patterns that encourage illness. Some of these patterns may include fibromyalgia, depression, addictions, low self-esteem, weight issues, being overly influenced by others, or even just shutting down.

> *As the oldest child, I felt responsible for my family. I took care of my siblings and even felt the need to save my mom and dad from their pain. My core behavior was "save everyone". Therefore I became overly responsible for everybody and established codependent patterns.* ~ Anne

> *I have a very bad temper. I grew up in a chaotic household. Both my mother and father were alcoholics. When they had too much to drink, they fought so intensely that*

they forgot I was even there. Sometimes I went and hid in my closet with my hands over my ears, fighting back tears.

I learned that holding everything in was not healthy. As an adult I would explode at the slightest difficulty. These tools help me to respond to stress with more patience and understanding. ~ Paul

I grew up every day of my life feeling like crying and not understanding why. Ever since I can remember, I could feel the emotions of parents, grandparents, siblings and others. Although I could feel the love from others, I also picked up on their dysfunctions, depression, stress, and anxiety. I sensed the severity of people's pain and trauma, as well as the behaviors that people are stuck on. ~ Anne

As a teenager, I struggled to have friends. I thought every-one was sensitive like me. I believed they had the same ability to know and feel the way I did.

Other kids were uncomfortable with this. They would not ignore me, but would not really be my friend. Find-ing a best friend was a challenge. I was sensitive to other's emotions and did not play their games. ~ Kay

2

Emotions are key signposts that help us navigate life

When you allow yourself to feel, you heal faster and experience life more fully. Life becomes a learning adventure rather than a road to nowhere. To be happy means to be healthy, whole and satisfied.

Emotions = Energy in Motion

Emotions are energies that like to move and flow. In other words, they don't like to be stuck. When they are blocked, they may cause emotional, mental or physical pain that can lead to dis-ease.

Your emotions can be key indicators or signs. When recognized, can help us to live a more centered and balanced life.

> *As a child, it was not accepted within my family to talk about my feelings. So I focused my emotional energy inside myself. This would later manifest as intestinal issues-specifically colitis.* ~ Kay

I can be very hard on myself. Since childhood, I have dealt with issues of perfectionism as a way of trying to avoid failure. This resulted in physical ailments, especially those involving my stomach and intestines. As time went on, I developed a lot of food sensitivities and allergies. I would go through periods of unhealthy weight loss. Since doing these exercises my digestion and overall health have improved immensely. ~ Eric

In my early 20's, I took drugs and alcohol. I got stuck on the joy and euphoria that they delivered. I eventually discovered when I could no longer afford the drugs and alcohol that I was looking for ways to numb myself. I had nowhere else to turn but to face my emotions. Excited, I found tools to help me grow. ~ Anne

4

Your network space; your energy field

Your energy field is a network of space that surrounds your body like a bubble with a range of 4-7 feet. The human energy field supplies your physical, emotional and mental bodies with information that you have acquired throughout life. When your network is clear, you feel focused, centered, freer and happier!

Your network may get wires crossed or have missing connections. Inside you, there might be a space with trapped emotions and/or memories.

You can feel weak and confused because the network that surrounds you is stuck or collapsed. Using the following exercises will help Repair, Rebuild and Reboot your Network.

As a sensitive person, your network can get sluggish. This can lead you to feel imbalanced and unstable. It's as if pieces of your true self are missing. When you allow the feelings of others to influence your space, your ability to make your own choices might be influenced. Sometimes the feelings can be so overwhelming, that it seems your network space is breaking down, shutting down or falling apart. You might numb yourself with addictions and denial.

In order to not be overwhelmed as a sensitive person, there are some key practices to help you maintain your balance. One of the most important is to acknowledge your pain. Two other keys include knowing how to move forward and learning how to move out of your stuck space. Emotions like to move and flow.

Emotions can be energy in motion

I was taking care of my husband when he was dying. Being sensitive, I took on his emotions, his mother's, his children's and his close friend's. My space felt overwhelmed with all the emotional clutter from others, and my network jammed. I was on the verge of a nervous breakdown. It created unhealthy relationships and resentment toward everyone I was dealing with. Using these exercises helped me cope. ~ Kay

When I became successful, people's attitude towards me changed. I would sometimes lie in bed crying alone, and wondering what I had done. It wasn't until someone said

"Don't you know that people might be jealous of you?" I began exploring not to take other people's insecurities too personally in my space ~ Anne

I was visiting a friend in the hospital. I began to sense a headache on top of my head. I sensed that she disapproved of something I had said. I began to slowly breathe below my navel, replant myself and clear out my space. Within a minute or two, the headache vanished. I did this while I was carrying on a conversation with her. ~ Eric

When you find yourself getting stuck as we all do from time to time, the Energetic Exercises will help (they have for us). By becoming conscious of your network/energy field, you can have more awareness of your need to feel centered and clear.

Being sensitive is a gift

Although being sensitive can sometimes feel like a burden, in actuality your sensitivity is a gift. You have the ability to see and feel more effectively the behaviors of others. While this can feel challenging, it increases your knowledge for yourself and those around you.

You can become more aware and listen to others without judgment. Your sensitivity can also be helpful in understanding why people react in certain ways.

Everyone came to me with their problems - it was as if I had the word therapist written on my forehead. I could easily sense what they were feeling, and often had the right answer to help them. I became grateful for my high level of sensitivity. Especially once I learned not to let their emotions or energy in my space. ~ Shawn

My Dad blacked out at home, then got back up and went to bed. I had a feeling that he may die. We called the ambulance and went to the hospital. His heart was

*continually stopping. After being in ICU, he received a
pacemaker and is still alive today at 88 years old. My sensitivity levels just knew that he was going to die if he did
not get medical help.* ~ Anne

*When I spontaneously proposed to my girlfriend, I told
her I did not have a ring. She agreed to marry me and
said she did not need a ring. I woke up the next day sens-
ing that having a ring was important to her. I spent the
next few weeks searching for one. When I finally surprised
her with an engagement ring, she realized all along that
she really did want one. I am so glad I listened to my
instincts.* ~ Eric

As a sensitive person you can tune into what it means to be
gifted. Can you remember a time when you listened to a piano
or a guitar that was tuned and played masterfully? Music played
with inspiration can move people to soar. Your sensitivity can
also be a springboard to help you live your life to the fullest.
The key is to allow yourself to feel, yet not let the emotions or
feelings get stuck in your space.

9

Men can be sensitive too

How many times have we heard the following statements?

Big boys don't cry.

Act like a man.

Come on, grow up.

Take it like a man.

Males are sensitive and want acknowledgment of their emotions. Boys are conditioned as to how they "should" act at an early age, with input from parents, friends and society. This conditioning can be painful and confusing. You see many young boys being affectionate and sensitive. But by the time they are 4 or 5 years old, society starts telling them "act like a man." At some point, family, parents, and society tell them that a boy's sensitive behavior is not OK.

In our exploration, many males want to be as in touch with their feelings and don't want to be denied their sensitivity. Often times it may be uncomfortable for them to express themselves.

Because of learned behaviors, many men are afraid to express their sensitivity. As young boys, they've picked up on many of society's cues and have learned that it's "wrong" to express their sensitivity.

When I was 34, my mom was killed in a car accident. Prior to her death, I hadn't cried in 15 years. I perceived from social conditioning that crying was considered weak, repulsive, shameful, and unacceptable for men to engage in, except under the most extreme of circumstances.

Instead, I buried my sensitivity with the result that my emotions and feelings were expressed with incredible rage and anger. Following my mom's auto accident and subsequent death 10 days later, I cried every day for over a month. As a man, I realized how healing and powerful crying is. Now I can shed tears over something as painful as a loss, to something as beautiful as music, or to something as joyful as looking into the eyes of my wife. ~ Eric

∞ ∞ ∞

I am back in the woods by my pond. I have my BB gun. I see a robin. I shoot and kill it. Walking over to the fallen bird, I start crying. Then I picked up the bird and held it for a long time just crying and looking at it.

Through this experience I realized the beauty of this bird and the loss of its life. Later, I gave the robin a burial

11

and cried more. Days later, I visited the gravesite and prayed for the bird that I killed. ~ Tom

As a child, I felt others' emotions and feelings so much that they overwhelmed me. It seemed I would absorb their pain in order to make them and myself feel better. Among male friends, this some times led to my being mistreated or ignored. Eventually, my resentment boiled to the point that I would engage them in an argument or a fistfight. ~ Eric

After joining the military, I found that men searched me out to listen to them. They valued my honesty and truthfulness. My awareness of others' needs, allowed me to support them during their difficult times. It was an interesting experience: being in a macho world of the military and utilizing my sensitive side. ~ Tom

As a mother, it broke my heart to see young boys break down in tears at competitive sports events. Many adults seem to put their own interest before the children's feelings,

leaving a child to feel weak and confused. The lack of understanding for what a child is experiencing caused an enormous amount of anger and/or loneliness for the child. I remember thinking why isn't anybody seeing these young boys cry and being unhappy? Why isn't anybody noticing and standing up for them? ~ Anne

∞ ∞ ∞

Over the years, men have learned to withhold tears and suppress their emotions. Their innate ability and desire to offer support and nurturing to others becomes stunted. In some cases, sensitivity is replaced with shame and anger. Consequently, many men are careful with whom they open up to and trust because of the fear of being rejected. Men may shut down if they feel they cannot be safe enough to express their feelings. Holding in feelings and emotions may lead to explosive reactions.

As more men have permission to be sensitive, these stereotypes about boys and men are being seen exactly for what they are: old, out-dated, self-limiting beliefs perpetuated by both men and women. In fact, many men these days are looking for women that don't expect them to be the hard Macho Man.

People can help transform these beliefs by helping to create a safe space for men to express themselves. Imagine men reclaiming their own sensitivity. The potential that the exercises offer in Answers For Sensitive People are keys that help inspire greater emotional stability.

Four energetic exercises to help you center and stay balanced

Now you're ready for the four basic Energetic Exercises that will help you create balance and harmony in your own energy system. These exercises are all immediately accessible to you, and if practiced, can assist you in feeling confident, centered and balanced. As a bonus, they also bring more freedom, fun, ease and joy into your life. For beginners, it is recommended to do these exercises in the seated position. The four exercises are:

1. Breathing

2. Planting

3. Clearing

4. Opening

Energetic Exercise 1: Breathing

The most important, immediately accessible tool you have is your own breath. It's been said that the most profound medicine for humans is produced in the body. What is this medicine? It's your own breath, your first and foremost ally. The power of breath cannot be underestimated.

You might be thinking, but I'm alive, I breathe every day and I still feel overwhelmed with all my feelings and experiences. The kind of breathing we are talking about is different. It's called belly breathing and has an amazing ability to calm the body and the mind.

Did you know that the health of every cell in your body depends on the oxygen carried through your bloodstream? How does that oxygen move? Through your breath.

Your breath scans the body. When you don't breathe through your belly, your breath cannot report important information back to the heart and brain. Belly breathing supports a healthy mind-body connection, creating optimum health.

> *I began having panic attacks after taking care of my father with Alzheimer's, working full-time and being a single mother of two children. The only thing that got me through this was my deep breathing.* ~ Anne

While working in the corporate world, bombarded with phone calls and constantly putting out fires, I used belly breathing to find that calm in the storm. Belly breathing helped me center and go back into my day feeling renewed. ~ Kay

∞ ∞ ∞

Energetic Exercise 1

◆ *Let's Breathe: This is How You Do It*

Basic Steps to Breathe from Your Lower Belly

1. Sitting or standing, close your eyes and place your hands, one on top of the other, on your lower belly. Note to beginners: closing your eyes can help you go deeper inside.

2. As you breathe in, feel your hands rise with every inhalation. As you breathe out, feel your hands fall with every exhalation.

BREATHE

inhale

exhale

3. Allow your breath to be smooth, slow, deep and gentle. Breathe in and breathe out through your nose in a controlled, continuous rhythm.

Try breathing this way for a minute. Can you feel the difference? Shallow breathing from your upper chest has been scientifically known to cause stress, anxiety and heart palpitations.

The more deeply you breathe, the healthier you will be.

◆ *Benefits of Belly Breathing*

- ❑ Calming

- ❑ Energizing

- ❑ Promotes clear, positive thinking

- ❑ Promotes circulation

- ❑ Cleanses your entire body, especially your lymphatic system which processes all the toxins in your body

- ❑ Reduces stress and anxiety

- ❑ Promotes healthy digestion and elimination

When you breathe low, you will be more in the flow.

Practice the deep belly breathing until you feel really comfortable with it. You don't need a specific place or time to practice this. You can practice while standing in a shopping line. Try practicing it for a minute or two lying in bed right before you go to sleep, and first thing in the morning before you get out of bed. The point is you can practice this any time during the day or while waiting in traffic.

Driving home from out of town I got caught in a blizzard. Behind me there was a semi truck and there was no where to go. I thought for sure I was going to die and the only thing that got me through this was deep breathing.

~ Anne

∞ ∞ ∞

Because your body was designed to breathe this way, if you practice belly breathing it will become your natural way of breathing. Check in occasionally to make sure that your breath is coming first from your lower belly. With practice, you will eventually notice how much calmer you feel.

Energetic Exercise 2: Planting

What is planting and does it assist you? Have you ever seen a seed become a big, strong, sturdy tree without sending deep roots into the ground? Planting helps anything become what it can be. It allows you to feel secure, present, and centered in your own energy. When you're deeply planted, you feel the strength of your own energy flowing and

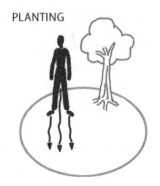

PLANTING

circulating, nurturing your body and mind. Planting helps you feel clear and alert, as if you were connecting to a continuous, vital energy source. Additionally, it helps you to feel more comfortable and confident in your own body.

> *I love to fantasize and daydream. Planting my body helps me focus more. I am able to be more present in conversations with others and less distracted.* ~ Yvonne

> *I feel so much more secure and stable when I plant roots into the earth. Like a tree, I can bend and flex but unpleasant situations are less likely to bowl me over. I have even noticed my self- confidence has improved.* ~ Shawn

> *I am less anxious to make changes in my life when I plant roots and connect with the earth. Although I may still feel lonely at times, I know that planting myself gives me comfort.* ~ Paul

Energetic Exercise 2

◆ *Let's Plant: This is How You Do It*

Easy Steps to Plant Your Roots Deep Into the Earth

1. Start with Exercise 1. Breathing – sitting or standing.

2. Close your eyes and bring your awareness down to the soles of your feet.

3. Imagine your favorite tree. Now imagine the roots of your favorite tree growing directly from the soles of your feet. You can even imagine roots also growing out of the base of your spine for added support.

4. Use your belly breathing to encourage your roots to grow as deep as they can into the Earth.

5. Feel, see, hear or sense yourself firmly planted.

6. Breathe your roots deeper expanding like a big strong sturdy tree.

Try taking a few moments each morning to start your day this way. Notice the difference it makes to your whole day. You can also plant your roots any time you feel off balance. You might be interested to see how planting your roots while standing in a shopping line, lying in bed, flying on a plane, driving in a car, or even when having a disagreement will help you to feel more stable.

What happens when you don't plant? Imagine a tree in a storm that isn't firmly rooted. It can come crashing down. This is what can happen to your energy system when you haven't planted your roots. When you're not planted, your life can seem out of control.

> *During a public hearing, an attorney began to question my credentials and experience. I found myself being very angry. Instead of letting him get control, I planted myself. I stated my case and position. I could tell the planning commission was paying more attention to what I was saying.* ~ Eric

∞ ∞ ∞

Several times a day, take a few moments to plant your roots deep into the earth. In fact, the more deeply you plant your roots, the more you can grow. By being firmly rooted, you move forward and accelerate your own growth.

**The more you can plant
the more you can grow**

**And if you can't grow, you can't go . . .
where your passions take you!**

Now that you're familiar with the first two Energetic Exercises, Breathing and Planting, it's time for the Clearing Exercise to help you have the space for what you want in your life.

Energetic Exercise 3: Clearing

Earlier we described your energy field as a network space and how it becomes cluttered and full of leftover emotions and experiences. This clutter holds us back and slows us down. The clearer and more open you can maintain your network space, the more access you have to clarity, healthy relationships, happiness, and joy. As you open up and clear the clutter, you create more space in which your dreams can become reality. By allowing your network to expand you create more space for abundance for anything you want.

The more space you clear,
The more room there is to create
to make your dreams comes true

◆ *What are we clearing? The clutter!*

What kinds of things have a tendency to get into your space, especially when you're sensitive?

CLEAR

❑ people's emotions, including those of coworkers, clients, family and friends

❑ old belief patterns

❑ opinions of mistakes

❑ stress

- ❏ anxiety
- ❏ fears
- ❏ worry
- ❏ shame
- ❏ guilt
- ❏ blame
- ❏ anger

Perhaps this example will help you understand what we mean. Imagine a spacious home built to your specific desires. Now imagine all of your coworkers, clients, colleagues and friends barging in through the front door uninvited. Each one brings along their emotional baggage, such as sorrow, pain, insecurities, jealousy, fear, etc. As all their baggage piles up, your beautiful home becomes unrecognizable and uncomfortable because there's so much clutter.

Now imagine this happening in your energy network. While you may not actually see all of this clutter and baggage filling up your space, you can certainly feel it. With all of this pressure, it's no wonder that sometimes you might feel depressed, anxious or stressed. It feels smothering and over whelming!

That's a signal that it's time to clear out your home, your energy network! If you do this exercise on a regular basis, you will feel healthier and less drained.

At the age of 25, my life had gotten to be too much for me. I was newly divorced, working full time, and living on my own for the first time in my life. I was also a sensitive

24

person carrying everyone else's stuff. But I did not know I was doing that. Because of all this, I was on and off anti-depressants.

The big step towards taking care of myself happened when I learned how to clear other people's energy from my space. As I did this, I also continued to learn new ways of taking care of myself. I kept on using these tools until I was able to break through being stuck. These energetic tools helped me. ~ Kay

I noticed I disliked large crowds, such as at sporting events and festivals. It's as if I was the one who was on stage and I could feel the mood and intensity of the crowd. It wasn't until Anne pointed out to me in a session that a particular sadness and despair I was feeling was not my own. Rather it was the energy I had picked up from a church festival the night before. From that point on, I realized how important it was for me to plant myself before mingling in a large crowd, and to clear myself once I left it. ~ Eric

Until I learned how to clear my space, I had a hard time being around my family. I picked up on their emotions

and carried them around feeling depressed, lonely and out of place. When I learned to clear my space, using these tools, I let go of their emotions much faster. ~ Anne

Energetic Exercise 3

◆ *Let's Clear: This is How You Do It*

Easy Steps to Clear and Expand Your Energy Field and Network Space

1. First do Energetic Exercises 1 & 2 Breathing/Planting Then close your eyes and bring your awareness to your own personal energy field that surrounds you.

2. With every deep breath you take, imagine your space expanding around you on all sides. Create the image of having arms pushing out the front, back, left side, right side, above your head and below your feet. You might imagine you are a beach ball or balloon opening up.

3. As your space expands, notice if there is clutter in your physical body and energy network around you. It might feel like heaviness or discomfort.

4. Use an imaginary vacuum cleaner to remove and release any clutter, anxiety, stress, anger or other people's energies. Release this into an imaginary trash can

underneath your feet. Allow Earth's energy to absorb and recycle this.

5. For something that is really stuck, use a magic eraser to delete and/or erase it.

6. Breathe and replant your body.

NOTE: Add this to "putting it all together"—there is a possibility that other emotions may release.

**The more you clear
the more you can hear
your own Heart sing.**

Now that you have cleared all the clutter from your personal space, it is time to open up and receive.

Energetic Exercise 4: Opening to Receive

There are a variety of images that can help with opening and receiving. Use whatever one feels right for you. We offer a few here, and perhaps you'll find a different one that works even better for you!

As a young girl I would love to lie in the middle of the yard and look at the clouds. I now know this is how I cleared myself and became open. Being in nature kept

*me alive. As I would lie on a pile of leaves and watch the
clouds, I allowed myself to receive the gifts of love and
peace. I became more in touch with who I am.*   ~ Anne

*My truck was getting old but I had limited funds to
replace it. Using these tools, I kept myself open for any
new opportunities. By coincidence, a complete stranger
told me my truck had been recalled for frame defects.
When the dealer inspected it, they found a defect.
I received 20 times the value of my vehicle. I will never
forget that staying open to possibilities helped magnetize
just what I needed.*   ~ Eric

*I spent 25 years giving to others. I forgot how to receive. I
realized that always giving was selfish because others wanted
the same opportunity of giving. When I allowed myself to
open up and receive, my life became fuller. After using these
tools, I gained a closer connection to spirit .*   ~ Anne

Energetic Exercise 4

◆ *Let's Receive: This is How You Do It*

Easy Steps to Open Up and Receive

RECEIVE

1. Do Energetic Exercises 1-3 Breathing/
Planting/Clearing

2. With your eyes closed, bring your awareness to the top of your head.

   a. Imagine your favorite flower. See and/
   or feel it opening up and fully blooming
   right on the top of your head. A golden sun just above
   your head encourages your flower to fully bloom.

      or

   b. Imagine a wooden door, right on the top of your head.
   Grab the handle of that wooden door, open it up.

      or

   c. Imagine your crown as the ceiling of a beautiful plan-
   etarium. As you push the button, the ceiling rolls back
   and opens to a beautiful starlit sky.

   Note: If you don't feel it opening, just use your intention.
   Intend to open to receive.

3. Once you've chosen your image, allow yourself to open
up and completely receive. Feel the inspiration, clarity

and joy, as you imagine a golden sun flowing into your crown. With each breath the sun flows into your entire physical body. Once your body is filled with light, continue to fill the energy network that surrounds you with golden sunlight.

4. Enjoy this space you have created.

Envision your crown open and receptive to inspiration, love, and joy that can create a different tone for your day. If practiced on a regular basis, you will notice yourself opening up to the wisdom and joy that naturally resides within you. You will find yourself having sudden moments of realization. These "Aha" moments or insights can enrich your life.

Putting it all together

When used daily, these Energetic Exercises can help reduce stress and clear stuck emotions. They also help you to embrace your sensitive nature and inspire your life in healthy ways. This means you can understand your sensitivity and manage your life with more awareness. What is awareness? A choice to see things the way they are so you can generate change if you choose

We have practiced these tools for years and have seen and experienced tangible results from their use. Admittedly, some days are more challenging than others. Sometimes we have had strong emotional releases involving crying, laughing, or fits of anger. Learning to go through this process with appreciation for your journey and lessons helps make your life more meaningful and alive. In order to gain the benefits of these Exercises, like any set of muscles, you've got to use them! We suggest at least on a daily basis, the more you use them the more fun they can be!

Breathe . . . life into your body.
Plant . . . your roots so your life can unfold.
Clear . . . the clutter.
Receive . . . your power and wisdom.

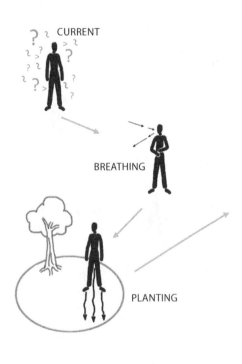

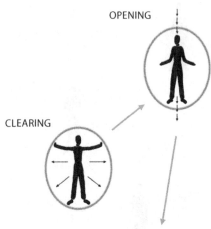

OPENING

CLEARING

RESULTS:
Improved health
More energy
Less drowning in emotions
More clarity
Happier
Strength to do the the things you want to do

◆ *What Kind of Results Can You Expect from Regularly Doing the Exercises?*

❑ Improved health

❑ More energy

❑ Less drowning in emotions

❑ More clarity

❑ Feeling happier

❑ More strength and courage to do the things you want to do

❑ Ability to make things happen in your life that you haven't been able to prior

❑ Ability to feel confident in groups

❑ Ability to go to school

❑ Ability to be calm

❑ Improved relationships

If you feel any amount of discomfort while doing these exercises, please consult your therapist and/or doctor.

About EnergeticAnswers.com

Our cutting-edge team offers a variety of services from medical intuitives, energy medicine, astrology, psychics, essential oils, yoga, angel readings, tarot cards, channeling, and much more.

While progressing into the 21st century, we continue to explore new avenues that connect us to unlimited possibilities. Our team has found that seeking new horizons and experiences with less seriousness can accelerate our growth and expansion. Join our unique team today!! Go to **www.EnergeticAnswers.com.**

Energetic Answers offers alternative answers which may not be found in traditional therapies. Medical Science is currently studying more of the well-known forms of "Biofield Therapy" and is finding them to have noticeable physiological effects. These studies consistently show changes in blood chemistry, heart rate, breathing and respiratory response. Studies done on the effects of Relaxation Response found it increases the antibodies found in the immune system. Less stress plays specific roles in fighting infection.

◆ *Results Are:*

❑ Pain relief

❑ Improved immune system

❑ Stress reduction and relaxation

❑ Acceleration of healing process

❑ Emotional and mental release and repair

◆ *Suggested Reading*

Psychic Psychology; Energy Skills for Life and Relationships. John Friedlander and Gloria Hemsher. North Atlantic Books. 2011

Basic Psychic Development. John Friedlander and Gloria Hemsher. Weiser Books. 1999

About the Authors

Anne Steffen-Russo created Energetic Answers. Anne is an internationally-known alternative therapist, medical intuitive, philosopher and author. She has traveled the world studying numerous natural healing methods. Finding answers for her own high levels of sensitivity, she enjoys educating others through her seminars and private sessions.

Kay Wise graduated from college, worked 30 years at the Procter & Gamble Co., followed by graduation from massage school. She was further educated by teachers from the Berkley Psychic Institute in California to enhance her natural skills and gifts. These experiences are all incorporated in Kay's current work of intuitive readings.

Eric Russo is the director of an environmental organization dedicated to promoting thoughtful hillside design and engineering. He is a reflexologist and an astrologer. Eric is a self-taught stone mason and carpenter.

Answers for Sensitive People is a hands-on, concise and easy-to-follow guide that holds appeal for a wide audience of readers. Whether you are a beginner in the area of self-help, or someone who has been through years of self-exploration and therapy, *Answers for Sensitive People* combines insight, empathy and practical advice.

This book will help you in three ways. First, the real-life stories demonstrate that you are not alone in your sensitivity. Second, the exercises provide practical and effective ways to comprehend, integrate and master high levels of sensitivity. Third, you will discover that your sensitivity is in fact a strength rather than a perceived weakness.

If you are searching for answers to your sensitivity, this book is a must read. Not only will you be feel more secure and empowered, you will become more adept at handling difficult situations, people, or the daily stress and demands of life. Likewise, you will develop a more neutral, compassionate and objective response to the sensitivity of others.

978-1-939324-01-6 $12.95

51295

9 781939 324016

Made in the USA
Las Vegas, NV
30 June 2023

74050563R00036